AI Tax Law, Compliance & Filing Rules

How Algorithms Stay Up-to-Date with IRS Regulations

By Joe Correa

Published by Live Stronger Faster

First Edition

Table of Contents

Introduction

The tax code was never designed for humans. It was designed for lawyers, lobbyists, accountants, and decades of political compromise layered on top of each other. Every year, tens of thousands of pages of IRS rules, regulations, revenue rulings, court cases, and administrative guidance are released, amended, repealed, reinterpreted, or quietly updated. The result is a system so complex that even trained professionals struggle to keep up. Ordinary taxpayers are expected to understand not only what they earned and spent, but how every dollar fits into a constantly shifting legal framework. This complexity is not accidental—it is structural. And in a system where complexity creates risk, fear becomes a powerful tool. People overpay taxes, avoid deductions, and hesitate to claim legitimate benefits because they are afraid of making a mistake. AI changes this equation completely.

Artificial intelligence does not "guess" at tax law. It reads it. It ingests entire bodies of tax code, IRS publications, Treasury regulations, court opinions, and administrative rulings. It continuously monitors changes in legislation, notices issued by the IRS, and new interpretations by tax authorities. Where humans rely on memory and manual updates, AI operates on real-time knowledge graphs. When Congress passes a bill at midnight, when the IRS issues emergency guidance, or when a court changes how a deduction is interpreted, AI systems can update their compliance engines in hours or even minutes. That means your tax strategy no longer depends on last year's rules or your accountant's recollection. It is always anchored to what the law actually says right now.

Compliance has traditionally been the most expensive part of taxes. Not because filing is difficult, but because knowing what is allowed and what is prohibited is hard. A single misclassified deduction can trigger penalties. A misapplied credit can result in audits. A reporting error can snowball into years of correspondence with the IRS. AI reduces this risk by turning law into logic. Every form, schedule, limitation, threshold, phase-out, and exception becomes part of a structured system that validates every entry before it is filed. Instead of hoping your return is correct, AI proves it. Every number is tested against current law, every rule is enforced automatically, and every risk is flagged before it becomes a problem.

One of the most powerful shifts AI brings to tax compliance is the move from static rules to dynamic interpretation. Traditional tax software is built on fixed logic trees. It works until the law changes. AI, on the other hand, understands language, relationships, and context. It reads IRS publications the way lawyers do. It interprets how a deduction applies to a specific taxpayer. It understands when two rules conflict and which one takes priority. It even learns from enforcement patterns, recognizing what types of returns the IRS is more likely to scrutinize. This means compliance is no longer just about following the letter of the law—it is about following how the law is actually applied.

In a digital IRS environment, compliance is becoming continuous rather than annual. The government already receives real-time data from employers, banks, payment processors, brokerage firms, and gig-economy platforms. The IRS often knows what you earned before you do. AI allows taxpayers to match that same speed. Income is reconciled automatically. Reporting discrepancies are caught instantly. Estimated taxes, withholding, and reporting requirements are adjusted in real time as your financial life changes. Instead of discovering problems months later when you file, AI ensures that compliance happens as money moves.

The fear of audits has always been rooted in uncertainty. People worry not because they did something wrong, but because they don't know whether what they did was allowed. AI removes that uncertainty. By modeling IRS rules exactly as the IRS applies them, AI systems can calculate audit risk before a return is filed. If a deduction is technically legal but historically high-risk, the system will tell you. If a reporting method is compliant but likely to be questioned, the system flags it. This gives taxpayers a level of visibility that was previously available only to high-end tax attorneys and corporate compliance teams.

What makes AI especially powerful in tax law is its ability to manage exceptions. The U.S. tax code is not built on simple yes-or-no rules. Almost every rule has carve-outs, special cases, income limits, phase-outs, geographic exceptions, and industry-specific treatments. Humans miss these constantly. AI does not. It maps every exception and applies them automatically based on your profile. Whether you are a gig worker, real estate investor, crypto trader, retiree, business owner, or international taxpayer, the system knows which rules apply to you and which ones don't. This eliminates both overpayment and under-compliance.

AI also creates something that has never existed in personal taxation: explainable compliance. Instead of simply telling you that a deduction is allowed or denied, the system can show you the exact IRS rule, publication, or legal authority behind the decision. You don't have to trust a black box. You can see the logic, the citations, and the regulatory basis for every line on your return. This not only builds confidence but also gives you documentation if you are ever questioned by the IRS. Another revolutionary change is how AI handles updates. In the past, tax professionals would attend seminars, read newsletters, and manually update their knowledge. Software companies would release patches once or twice a year. With AI, updates are continuous. Legislative changes, emergency tax relief, disaster-area extensions, new credit programs, and compliance deadlines are reflected almost immediately. If the IRS changes how mileage is calculated, how crypto is reported, or how digital payments are taxed, your AI system knows before your next transaction posts.

This level of compliance does more than prevent mistakes—it creates strategic advantage. When you know exactly what the law allows, you can structure your income, investments, and expenses to stay within the safest and most favorable interpretations. You can move money, claim benefits, and time transactions with precision. Compliance stops being a burden and becomes a tool. You are no longer reacting to tax law; you are navigating it.

In this book, you will learn how AI systems read and apply tax law, how compliance engines are built, how real-time regulation tracking works, and how digital filing rules are enforced automatically. You will see how algorithms detect risks before the IRS does, how they validate every number on your return, and how they adapt instantly when laws change.

You will also understand how the future IRS will interact with AI-powered taxpayers in a fully digital, automated compliance ecosystem.

The old tax world was built on paperwork, fear, and human error. The new tax world is built on data, automation, and intelligence. AI does not replace the law—it makes the law usable. It turns thousands of pages of regulations into something that works for you instead of against you. By the time you finish this book, you will understand how compliance becomes effortless when algorithms do what humans were never meant to do: read, remember, and apply every rule, every time.

Chapter 1

How AI Reads, Interprets & Enforces Tax Law

Tax law is not a list of simple instructions. It is a living system made up of statutes passed by Congress, regulations written by the Treasury Department, interpretations issued by the IRS, and court rulings that redefine how every rule is applied. For decades, this legal maze has been navigated by humans who specialize in memorizing fragments of it while relying on outdated software and printed manuals to fill in the gaps. Artificial intelligence changes this completely by transforming tax law into a continuously updated, machine-readable system that is always current, always consistent, and always precise. Instead of relying on annual updates, AI systems ingest new laws, notices, revenue rulings, and court decisions in real time, converting them into structured rules that govern every calculation, validation, and filing decision.

At the core of an AI tax compliance system is something called a legal knowledge graph. This is a massive interconnected map of every tax rule and how it relates to every other rule. Deductions are linked to income types, filing statuses, income limits, documentation requirements, and audit triggers. Credits are tied to eligibility thresholds, residency rules, dependent qualifications, and expiration dates. AI does not store tax law as text—it stores it as relationships. When you enter a number on your tax return, the AI does not simply accept it; it evaluates that number against thousands of legal constraints instantly. If something violates the law, it is flagged before it ever reaches the IRS.

Unlike traditional tax software, which uses fixed logic trees written by programmers months or years earlier, AI systems can interpret legal language directly. They read IRS publications, Treasury regulations, and court decisions using natural language processing models trained on legal text. This allows AI to understand not just what a rule says, but what it means. When the IRS changes the definition of a business expense, when a new credit is introduced, or when a court reinterprets a long-standing rule, the AI updates its understanding without needing a software patch. It is essentially a living tax professional that never forgets and never falls behind.

One of the most powerful features of AI-driven tax law is its ability to handle ambiguity. Many tax rules contain phrases like "reasonable," "ordinary," "necessary," or "substantial," which require interpretation. Humans make judgment calls based on experience. AI makes them based on data. It analyzes how the IRS has enforced similar cases in the past, how courts have ruled, and how audit patterns have developed. It then assigns risk scores to different interpretations. This means you can choose whether to be conservative, moderate, or aggressive in how you apply the law, with full visibility into the potential consequences of each choice.

AI also enforces compliance by validating documentation. When you claim a deduction, the system knows what proof is required. Receipts, mileage logs, depreciation schedules, and income statements are automatically matched to the claim. If something is missing or inconsistent, the AI will not allow the return to proceed. This eliminates one of the most common causes of IRS problems: incomplete or poorly supported filings. Compliance is no longer about hoping you have the right paperwork; it is about having a system that refuses to let you file without it.

Another critical advantage of AI is its ability to detect contradictions. Human filers often make errors by entering information that conflicts across different forms. Income reported on one schedule does not match another. Deductions exceed allowable limits. Filing status conflicts with dependency claims. AI sees all of this instantly. It runs thousands of internal consistency checks that no human could perform manually. The result is a return that is not only legally compliant but internally coherent, which dramatically reduces the chance of IRS scrutiny.

As tax authorities move toward fully digital enforcement, AI becomes even more powerful. The IRS already uses its own algorithms to identify discrepancies, underreporting, and fraud. When taxpayers use AI to prepare their returns, they are effectively matching the IRS at its own technological level. Instead of being surprised by audits, they can see the same risks the IRS sees. Compliance becomes proactive instead of reactive, and fear is replaced by certainty.

By the end of this chapter, you should understand that AI does not simplify tax law by ignoring complexity. It simplifies it by mastering complexity. Every rule, exception, and interpretation becomes part of a unified system that works for you, not against you. This is the foundation of modern tax compliance, and it is the engine that makes everything else in this series possible.

"The Day the IRS Stopped Scaring People"

When Michael first opened the letter from the IRS, his hands started to shake. Even though it was just a routine notice about a missing form, years of anxiety rushed back instantly. He remembered the audit his father went through when he was a teenager, the stacks of paper, the endless phone calls, and the feeling of being guilty until proven innocent. Michael had done everything right this year, but fear didn't care about facts. It lived in the uncertainty.

Instead of panicking, Michael opened the AI tax app he had started using six months earlier. The moment he uploaded the IRS notice, the system analyzed it, cross-referenced it with his filed return, and pulled the exact rule that applied. The notice was triggered because a brokerage had sent a corrected 1099 after his return was submitted. The AI already had it. The IRS simply hadn't processed it yet. A green checkmark appeared on the screen, and a message told him that no action was required.

Michael sat back in his chair, stunned. For the first time in his adult life, the IRS had lost its power over him. There was nothing to argue, nothing to guess, nothing to fear. The AI knew the rules better than any human ever could, and it knew exactly how they applied to him.

Over the next few months, Michael watched how the system worked behind the scenes. Every time a new tax rule was announced, the AI updated itself automatically. When Congress changed depreciation schedules, his future tax projections adjusted. When the IRS issued guidance on crypto reporting, his investment dashboard adapted. He wasn't reacting to tax law anymore; he was living inside it, with perfect visibility.

One day, Michael's friend Sarah called him in a panic. She had just received a massive tax bill from the IRS for unreported freelance income. Michael invited her over and had her upload her financial data into his AI system. Within minutes, it identified several deductions she had missed, expenses that were misclassified, and income that had been double-counted by payment platforms. The AI recalculated everything and generated a corrected return that reduced her bill by more than half, all while staying fully compliant.

Sarah stared at the screen in disbelief. "Why doesn't everyone have this?" she asked.

Michael smiled. "They will."

As the years went on, the IRS itself became more automated. Audits were triggered by algorithms. Notices were sent by machines. But so were responses. Taxpayers armed with AI no longer feared the system. They understood it. Compliance became a quiet background process instead of a yearly nightmare.

The day finally came when Michael realized he hadn't thought about taxes in months. Not because he was ignoring them, but because AI had turned them into something predictable, transparent, and manageable. The fear that had haunted generations was gone, replaced by something far more powerful: certainty. And in a world where the rules never stop changing, certainty became the greatest financial advantage of all.

Chapter 2

Real-Time IRS Rule Tracking & Continuous Compliance

The greatest weakness of the traditional tax system has always been timing. Laws change, but people file once per year. Guidance is issued, but taxpayers learn about it months later. Penalties are assessed even when violations were unknowingly caused by rule updates that happened after income was earned. Artificial intelligence eliminates this time gap by turning tax compliance into a live, continuously updated system. Instead of freezing the law in time when you file, AI keeps your tax profile synchronized with the current IRS rulebook every day of the year.

At the heart of this system is real-time regulatory ingestion. AI platforms constantly monitor Congress, the Treasury Department, the IRS, federal courts, and even state agencies for any change that affects taxation. New bills, temporary relief programs, disaster extensions, credit adjustments, reporting thresholds, and filing rules are immediately pulled into the AI's knowledge base. The moment a new rule is published, it becomes part of how every transaction is evaluated. There is no lag, no waiting period, and no need for manual updates. This allows AI to maintain what is called continuous compliance. Every paycheck, bank deposit, crypto trade, rental payment, or freelance invoice is evaluated using the current tax code the moment it happens. If a reporting threshold changes, the AI recalculates your obligations instantly. If a deduction becomes restricted or expanded, your financial projections adjust automatically. You are never out of sync with the law because the law itself is always running inside your tax system.

One of the most important outcomes of this is that tax surprises disappear. Owing a large balance at tax time is almost always the result of outdated withholding, misestimated quarterly payments, or changes in the law that were not accounted for. AI prevents this by forecasting taxes using the latest rules every day. If you start earning more, it adjusts your withholding. If credits are phased out, it tells you immediately. If a new tax law increases or reduces your future liability, you see it before it affects you.

Real-time compliance also protects you from accidental violations. Many tax penalties come not from fraud but from timing mistakes, missing filings, or incorrect thresholds. AI knows when forms are due, when payments are required, and when disclosures are triggered. It alerts you before deadlines, not after. It files extensions automatically when needed. It even generates compliance checklists for complex situations like moving, starting a business, investing, or retiring. Nothing slips through the cracks because the system never stops watching.

Another critical advantage is how AI handles emergency tax changes. When disasters, pandemics, or economic crises occur, tax laws are often changed quickly. Deadlines are extended. Penalties are waived. Credits are introduced. Humans often miss these changes or learn about them too late. AI does not. It integrates emergency guidance immediately and applies it to your account. If you qualify for relief, the system knows. If your filing deadline changes, it updates your schedule. Compliance becomes adaptive rather than rigid.

AI also creates a full audit trail of compliance. Every rule that was applied, every threshold that was used, and every decision that was made is recorded with a timestamp and a source. If the IRS ever questions a filing, the AI can produce a complete compliance log showing exactly which law was in effect at the time and how it was applied. This transforms audits from adversarial battles into data-driven verifications.

As the IRS continues to modernize, real-time compliance will become the standard. The government is moving toward continuous reporting, automated matching, and digital enforcement. Taxpayers who use AI will not be at a disadvantage in this world—they will be ahead of it. They will know what the IRS knows, when it knows it, and how it applies to them.

Continuous compliance is not just a technical upgrade. It is a fundamental shift in power. When you always know where you stand with the tax system, fear disappears. Control returns. AI does not make the law simpler—it makes it visible, immediate, and manageable. And in a world of constant change, that visibility becomes the foundation of financial security.

"The System That Never Slept"

Alicia used to dread tax season like a yearly storm. No matter how careful she was, something always went wrong. A missing form. A late payment. A changed rule she didn't know about. But everything changed the day she connected her finances to an AI compliance system.

At first, she barely noticed it. Paychecks went in, expenses went out, and the AI quietly updated her tax projections in the background. But then a new federal tax credit was announced for energy-efficient home upgrades. Alicia was planning to replace her windows, and the AI immediately notified her that if she did it before December, she would qualify for a larger credit. It even adjusted her tax forecast to show the savings.

A month later, her freelance income increased, and the system automatically recalculated her estimated taxes. Instead of being shocked by a big bill later, her withholding and quarterly payments adjusted automatically. Alicia didn't have to do anything. The system never slept.

When wildfires hit her state, the IRS announced emergency extensions for affected areas. Alicia didn't even know about it until the AI notified her that her filing deadline had been moved. Her stress vanished instantly. While everyone else was scrambling to understand the new rules, her compliance was already updated.

One evening, her brother called in panic. He had just learned he owed thousands in penalties for a missed reporting requirement on his crypto trades. Alicia invited him over and connected his accounts to her AI system. Within minutes, it identified where he had missed filings, which penalties could be waived, and how to correct everything under current IRS guidance. What had felt like a disaster became a manageable fix.

Alicia realized something powerful: the IRS no longer operated in the shadows for her. Every rule, every change, every obligation was visible. She was no longer reacting to the tax system—she was synchronized with it.

In a world where laws changed faster than humans could track them, Alicia had something better than luck. She had a system that never slept, never forgot, and never let her fall behind.

Chapter 3

Audit-Proof Filing, Risk Scoring & IRS-Grade Validation

For most taxpayers, the greatest fear surrounding taxes is not the amount they owe, but the possibility of being audited. The audit process is intimidating, time-consuming, and emotionally exhausting because it places the burden of proof on the taxpayer. Even when people follow the rules, they often lack the documentation or clarity to defend themselves. Artificial intelligence changes this dynamic by turning every tax return into a fully validated, audit-ready financial record before it is ever submitted. Instead of hoping the IRS accepts your return, AI ensures that your filing meets the same analytical standards the IRS itself uses to evaluate risk.

At the core of AI-driven audit protection is risk scoring. The IRS uses sophisticated algorithms to decide which returns deserve closer inspection. These systems analyze income patterns, deduction ratios, industry averages, transaction histories, filing behaviors, and discrepancies between third-party data and taxpayer reports. AI tax platforms mirror this process. Every return is evaluated against IRS-style risk models before filing. If something looks unusual, inconsistent, or statistically out of line, the system flags it instantly. This allows taxpayers to correct, document, or restructure entries before they become a problem.

AI does not simply detect risk; it quantifies it. Each deduction, credit, income source, and reporting choice is assigned a risk score based on how likely it is to trigger IRS scrutiny. A business expense that is common and well-documented might have a low score. A rare or unusually large deduction might have a higher one. This gives taxpayers unprecedented visibility into how the IRS is likely to view their return. Instead of guessing whether something is "safe," they can see it in data-driven terms and decide how aggressive or conservative they want to be.

Another powerful feature of AI-driven compliance is validation against third-party reporting. The IRS receives copies of W-2s, 1099s, brokerage statements, crypto exchange reports, and payment processor data. AI tax systems pull in the same data. Every dollar you report is matched against what the IRS already has. If there is a discrepancy, it is identified before filing. This eliminates one of the most common causes of audits: mismatched income reporting. You are no longer surprised by IRS letters months later because the AI already reconciled everything in advance.

AI also performs what can be called forensic consistency checks. It looks for internal contradictions that humans often miss. If your income supports a certain lifestyle but your deductions suggest something else, the system flags it. If your business expenses don't align with your industry profile, the system asks for clarification. If depreciation schedules conflict with asset purchases, the system resolves it. These checks mirror the way IRS examiners think, which means your return is prepared as if it were already being audited.

Perhaps the most revolutionary aspect of AI-based tax filing is documentation automation. Every deduction, credit, and reporting decision is automatically linked to supporting evidence. Receipts, logs, statements, and records are attached digitally and stored in a secure compliance vault. If the IRS ever questions a line on your return, the AI can instantly produce the documentation and legal basis for it. There is no scrambling, no searching through emails, and no panic. Everything is already there.

AI also builds legal defensibility into your return. For each tax position you take, the system can cite IRS publications, Treasury regulations, and court rulings that support it. This creates what professionals call "substantial authority," which can protect you from penalties even if the IRS later disagrees with your interpretation. Your return becomes not just a set of numbers, but a legally reasoned financial statement. As digital enforcement becomes more powerful, this level of preparation becomes essential. The IRS is not just looking for mistakes; it is looking for patterns. AI allows you to see those patterns before the IRS does and adjust accordingly. It transforms audits from unpredictable threats into manageable, data-driven processes.

Audit-proof filing does not mean you will never be questioned. It means that if you are, you will be ready. With AI, every return is prepared as if it were going to be audited. And when you operate at that level of precision, fear disappears, replaced by confidence and control.

"The Return That Couldn't Be Broken"

Daniel had always done his own taxes, but every year felt like walking on thin ice. He ran a small online business, invested in crypto, and owned a rental property. Nothing illegal, but complicated enough to make him nervous. When a friend recommended an AI tax system, Daniel decided to try it, not because he expected miracles, but because he wanted peace of mind.

As he uploaded his financial data, the AI immediately started analyzing everything. It flagged one unusually high home-office deduction and showed him how it compared to

IRS averages for his type of business. It wasn't illegal, but it was risky. The system suggested an alternative method that was still compliant but less likely to raise red flags. Daniel accepted the recommendation.

Next, it reconciled all of his crypto trades with exchange reports. A small discrepancy appeared, something Daniel had never noticed. The AI corrected it before the return was filed. Then it linked every rental expense to a receipt, every depreciation claim to an asset record, and every income stream to a third-party report.

When the return was finished, Daniel didn't just see a refund number. He saw a risk score. It was lower than average. For the first time, he knew exactly where he stood.

Six months later, the IRS sent him a notice. His heart jumped, but when he uploaded it to the AI, the system showed him it was a routine inquiry about rental depreciation. With one click, it generated a full response package, including schedules, receipts, and legal citations. Daniel sent it off.

Two weeks later, the case was closed.

Daniel realized that the return hadn't survived the IRS—it had anticipated it. The system had prepared his finances the way the IRS would analyze them. His taxes weren't just filed. They were fortified.

And for the first time in his life, the IRS no longer felt like an enemy. It felt like a test he was already prepared to pass.

Chapter 4

Automated Filing Accuracy, Error Prevention & Zero-Defect Returns

Tax filing errors rarely come from dishonesty. They come from overload. Too many forms, too many rules, too many exceptions, and too many numbers moving at the same time. Humans were never designed to manually reconcile dozens of schedules, cross-reference third-party reports, calculate phaseouts, apply changing thresholds, and ensure consistency across an entire return. Artificial intelligence solves this problem not by simplifying the tax code, but by enforcing perfection at scale. AI-driven filing systems are built to prevent errors before they exist, creating what can best be described as zero-defect tax returns.

Automated accuracy begins with data normalization. Every source of financial information—W-2s, 1099s, bank feeds, payroll systems, brokerage statements, crypto exchanges, rental platforms, and payment processors—arrives in different formats. AI standardizes this data instantly, aligning it to IRS reporting structures and validating it against official schemas. If a number is malformed, duplicated, missing, or inconsistent, the system flags it before calculations begin. This ensures that errors are eliminated at the source rather than corrected later through amendments or audits.

Once data is normalized, AI applies layered validation logic. Each line item on a tax return is tested against multiple rules simultaneously. Mathematical accuracy is checked first. Then legal limits are enforced. Income thresholds, deduction caps, credit phaseouts, and filing status requirements are applied in real time. Traditional software often checks these sequentially, which allows compound errors to slip through. AI checks them holistically, meaning no number is ever evaluated in isolation. Every entry must make sense mathematically, legally, and contextually at the same time.

One of the most powerful aspects of AI accuracy is cross-form reconciliation. Many IRS issues arise because numbers technically add up but do not align across schedules. Income on one form does not match another. Adjustments conflict with deductions. Credits are calculated correctly but applied incorrectly. AI sees the entire return as a single system. If one number changes, the impact is propagated everywhere automatically. This eliminates silent errors that humans rarely catch until the IRS does.

AI also prevents filing errors caused by outdated assumptions. Taxpayers often rely on prior-year behavior, assuming the same rules still apply. AI does not assume. It verifies. Every rule used in the return is pulled from the current tax year's authority. If a deduction was eliminated, restricted, expanded, or redefined, the system enforces the new rule automatically. There is no risk of filing under old law because old law simply no longer exists inside the system.

Another major source of errors is form selection. Many taxpayers file the wrong forms or omit required schedules without realizing it. AI determines required forms dynamically based on activity, not user input. If you trade crypto, the appropriate disclosures are added. If you own rental property, the correct schedules appear. If you qualify for a credit, the system generates the supporting forms automatically. Filing completeness is enforced by design, not by memory.

AI also handles rounding, thresholds, and edge cases with extreme precision. Many IRS penalties arise from seemingly small discrepancies—amounts rounded incorrectly, thresholds exceeded by a few dollars, or calculations performed using the wrong base. AI tracks precision at every step. It knows when rounding is allowed, when it is prohibited, and how the IRS expects numbers to be presented. This level of accuracy dramatically reduces notices, delays, and rejections.

Perhaps the most overlooked benefit of AI filing accuracy is amendment prevention. Filing an amended return is costly, stressful, and often unnecessary if the original return had been prepared correctly. AI systems simulate post-filing IRS checks before submission. If something would likely generate a notice, the system treats it as an error and forces resolution before filing. This shifts corrections upstream, where they are cheap and painless, instead of downstream, where they are expensive and stressful.

In the end, automated accuracy is not about speed, though AI is fast. It is about certainty. A zero-defect return is one where every number is intentional, every rule is applied correctly, and every form tells the same story. When accuracy becomes automatic, compliance becomes effortless. And when compliance becomes effortless, taxes stop being a source of anxiety and start being just another background system running quietly in your favor.

"The Return That Fixed Itself"

Ethan had filed his taxes late three times in the past five years, not because he was irresponsible, but because every year his finances got more complicated. Promotions at work, a side consulting business, investment accounts, stock compensation, and a short-term rental had turned his tax return into something that felt dangerous. Every number he entered felt like it could be wrong. Every click felt permanent. He didn't fear paying taxes. He feared making a mistake he wouldn't discover until it was too late.

The first time Ethan used an AI tax system, he expected it to feel like upgraded software. What he didn't expect was that it felt like a living system that refused to let him fail. As soon as he connected his accounts, the AI began cleaning the data. Duplicate income entries were identified and merged. Expenses were categorized and re-categorized when better classifications were found. Numbers adjusted themselves as new information arrived. Ethan watched as totals changed, not randomly, but logically, as if the return were assembling itself.

When he manually entered an expense that exceeded an allowable limit, the system didn't reject it outright. Instead, it explained why the amount triggered a rule, showed the relevant IRS threshold, and offered compliant alternatives. Ethan realized something unsettling and comforting at the same time: the system wasn't waiting for him to be wrong. It was actively preventing it.

As the return grew, so did the complexity. The AI added schedules Ethan didn't even know existed. It linked depreciation from prior years automatically. It adjusted credits based on income phaseouts Ethan had never calculated correctly before. Each time a number changed, the entire return recalculated instantly, ensuring nothing broke downstream. The return wasn't static—it was adaptive.

One night, exhausted, Ethan accidentally entered an extra zero on a charitable contribution. In the past, that mistake would have followed him straight to the IRS. This time, the system paused. It flagged the amount as statistically abnormal, cross-checked it against prior years, and asked for confirmation. When Ethan corrected it, the system recalculated everything without a trace of the error ever existing.

As filing day approached, Ethan expected anxiety. Instead, he felt something new: calm. The AI ran a final pre-submission validation, simulating IRS checks one last time. It confirmed internal consistency, third-party matching, legal compliance, and documentation completeness. Only when everything passed did the "File" button become available.

Months later, when friends complained about IRS notices and amended returns, Ethan realized something remarkable had happened. His return hadn't survived tax season. It had eliminated the possibility of failure before it even began.

For the first time, taxes were not something Ethan endured once a year. They were something his system quietly handled with precision, correcting itself long before mistakes could ever become consequences.

And in that silence—free of letters, penalties, and fear—Ethan discovered what zero-defect compliance really felt like.

Chapter 5

AI Documentation, Digital Proof & Bulletproof Recordkeeping

For decades, tax compliance has depended not only on what was reported, but on what could be proven. The IRS does not operate on trust; it operates on evidence. Receipts, logs, statements, contracts, invoices, mileage records, depreciation schedules, and correspondence all form the backbone of defensible tax filings. The problem is not that taxpayers fail to generate this documentation, but that they fail to preserve, organize, and connect it properly. Artificial intelligence fundamentally transforms this process by turning documentation from an afterthought into a continuously generated, automatically linked compliance system.

Traditional recordkeeping relies on human discipline. Files must be saved, folders labeled, receipts scanned, logs maintained, and documents retained for years. Any break in this chain creates vulnerability. AI removes this fragility by capturing documentation at the moment financial activity occurs. When income is earned, the source is logged automatically. When an expense is incurred, the receipt is categorized, timestamped, and attached to the relevant tax category. When assets are purchased, depreciation schedules are generated instantly. Nothing is left to memory, intention, or habit.

AI-driven documentation systems operate on the principle of contextual evidence. A receipt is not just stored—it is understood. The system knows what the expense was for, how it relates to income, which deduction it supports, and what IRS rule governs its treatment. This context allows AI to reject invalid documentation before it becomes a liability. If a receipt does not meet substantiation requirements, the system flags it immediately. If a log is incomplete, the system requests correction. Documentation quality is enforced in real time, not questioned years later.

One of the most powerful capabilities of AI recordkeeping is its ability to maintain audit-ready documentation continuously. Every tax position taken on a return is linked to supporting evidence and legal authority. If the IRS ever questions a deduction, the AI can produce a complete documentation package instantly, including receipts, explanations, and citations. This transforms audits from chaotic document hunts into structured verifications. The burden of proof no longer feels overwhelming because it has already been met.

AI also enforces retention rules automatically. Different documents must be kept for different periods depending on their tax relevance. Humans forget these rules. AI does not. Records are retained, archived, or purged according to IRS guidelines without user intervention. This reduces both risk and clutter, ensuring compliance without unnecessary data hoarding.

Another critical advancement is AI's ability to correlate documentation across years. Many tax positions depend on historical records: carryforward losses, depreciation schedules, basis calculations, and prior elections. AI maintains continuity across tax years, ensuring that nothing is lost or misapplied. This eliminates one of the most common audit problems: missing historical documentation.

As tax enforcement becomes increasingly digital, documentation quality will matter more than ever. The IRS is moving toward automated audits where responses are evaluated by algorithms before humans ever see them. AI-prepared documentation speaks the same language as these systems. It is structured, complete, and precise. In this environment, recordkeeping is no longer a defensive chore—it is an active compliance strategy.

AI does not just store proof. It builds it. And when proof becomes automatic, compliance becomes unbreakable.

"The Box They Never Asked For"

For most of her adult life, Linda kept a cardboard box in the back of her closet labeled "Taxes." Inside were faded receipts, old bank statements, handwritten notes, and documents she barely remembered creating. Every year, she added to it, promising herself she would organize it someday. And every year, she didn't. The box was her insurance policy, her quiet reassurance that if the IRS ever came calling, she had something—anything—to show them.

The letter arrived on a Tuesday morning. The IRS was requesting documentation for deductions claimed three years earlier. Linda's stomach dropped. She pulled the box from the closet and opened it for the first time in years. The smell of old paper filled the room. Receipts had faded. Ink had smudged. Dates were missing. Some documents belonged to the wrong year. Others made no sense at all.

Panic set in.

A friend suggested she try an AI compliance platform before responding. Skeptical but desperate, Linda uploaded what she had. The system didn't scold her. It didn't judge her. It analyzed everything. It identified which documents were usable, which were insufficient, and which were irrelevant. Then it did something unexpected—it showed her what was missing and why.

The AI explained that some deductions required proof she no longer had, but others were fully defensible with records already stored digitally by banks and vendors. It pulled transaction histories, reconstructed expense logs, and matched payments to vendors automatically. For the first time, Linda saw her finances not as chaos, but as a structured system.

As she worked through the process, Linda realized something profound. The system wasn't just responding to the audit—it was rebuilding her entire recordkeeping foundation. Every document was labeled, linked, and stored in a secure vault. Every deduction was tied to evidence and legal authority. The box in her closet was becoming obsolete in real time.

When the response package was complete, it wasn't a stack of random papers. It was a clean, organized digital file with explanations, timelines, and citations. Linda submitted it with a trembling click.

Weeks passed. Then months.

The IRS closed the inquiry without adjustment.

Linda sat in her living room, staring at the empty space where the box used to be. She had thrown it away. From that day forward, everything changed. Every receipt went straight into the system. Every expense was logged automatically. Every financial decision came with instant documentation. The fear she had carried for decades evaporated quietly, replaced by confidence.

Years later, when another IRS letter arrived—routine, automated, harmless—Linda smiled. She uploaded it to the system and watched as the AI prepared a response she didn't even need to send.

The box they never asked for was gone forever.

And with it, the anxiety that had weighed on her for most of her life.

Chapter 6

AI-Guided Responses, Automated Correspondence & Surviving IRS Notices

For most taxpayers, the moment an IRS notice arrives is the moment control disappears. The language feels intimidating, the deadlines feel urgent, and the consequences feel unclear. Even simple notices can trigger panic because they imply error, scrutiny, or punishment. In reality, the majority of IRS correspondence is automated, procedural, and correctable. Artificial intelligence changes how these interactions unfold by transforming IRS communication from a reactive crisis into a structured, guided process that is calm, precise, and defensible from the very first response.

AI-driven correspondence begins with classification. When a notice arrives, the system does not treat it as a threat—it treats it as data. The notice is scanned, parsed, and categorized according to IRS notice codes, issue types, tax years involved, and required actions. Whether the notice relates to income mismatch, documentation requests, penalty assessments, missing forms, or payment discrepancies, the AI instantly understands what the IRS is asking and why. This eliminates confusion and prevents incorrect or incomplete responses, which often escalate minor issues into major problems.

Once classified, the AI evaluates the notice against the taxpayer's existing compliance record. Because documentation, filings, and legal justifications are already stored and linked, the system can determine whether the IRS is correct, partially correct, or incorrect. If the notice is generated due to delayed third-party reporting, processing lag, or automated mismatch, the AI identifies this immediately. If correction is required, the system determines whether it should be handled through explanation, documentation submission, amendment, or appeal. This decision is made based on IRS procedure—not emotion.

One of the most powerful advantages of AI-guided responses is precision timing. IRS deadlines are rigid, and missed responses often result in automatic penalties or escalation. AI systems track deadlines continuously and generate response timelines automatically. If an extension is available, the system applies it. If immediate response is required, the system prioritizes action. This removes one of the most common taxpayer failures: doing nothing because they do not know what to do.

AI also generates correspondence in the language the IRS expects. Human responses often fail because they are emotional, verbose, or legally vague. AI-generated responses are structured, factual, and aligned with IRS procedural standards. Each response includes references to applicable rules, supporting documentation, and clear explanations that address the specific issue raised. This dramatically increases the likelihood of resolution without further inquiry.

Another critical function of AI correspondence is escalation control. Not every notice should be fought. Some should be accepted and resolved quickly. Others require pushback. AI evaluates the cost, risk, and probability of success for each path and recommends the optimal response strategy. This prevents unnecessary disputes while ensuring that legitimate positions are defended properly.

AI also maintains a complete communication log. Every notice, response, attachment, and IRS interaction is stored with timestamps and references. If a case escalates, this log becomes invaluable. It shows compliance, responsiveness, and consistency—qualities the IRS values highly. This recordkeeping also protects taxpayers from repeated requests for the same information, a common frustration in long-running cases.

As the IRS continues to automate enforcement and correspondence, AI-guided communication becomes essential. Automated systems respond best to structured, precise inputs. AI speaks that language fluently. It does not argue emotionally or speculate—it responds with evidence, logic, and compliance.

Surviving IRS notices is no longer about resilience or luck. It is about preparation. With AI, every notice becomes a manageable task instead of a destabilizing event. Control returns to the taxpayer not because the IRS becomes less powerful, but because the taxpayer finally operates with the same level of precision and structure.

"The Letter That Didn't Ruin His Weekend"

The envelope arrived on a Friday afternoon, just as Marcus was packing up his office to head home. He recognized it instantly. Government issue. Official font. The kind of envelope that used to sit unopened on his desk for hours while dread slowly crept in. For most of his adult life, IRS letters had ruined weekends, vacations, and sleep. This one should have done the same.

But it didn't.

Marcus opened the letter, scanned it with his phone, and uploaded it into his AI compliance system without sitting back down. He didn't reread it ten times. He didn't search online forums. He didn't call anyone in a panic. He simply let the system work.

Within seconds, the AI classified the notice. CP2000. Income mismatch. Automated. Non-audit. Marcus felt his shoulders relax slightly. The system explained that a payment processor had reported gross income without accounting for refunded transactions. This was common. Correctable. Not personal.

The AI pulled the relevant records instantly. Refund logs. Bank deposits. Processor statements. Everything aligned perfectly. The discrepancy wasn't Marcus's mistake—it was a timing issue between reporting systems. The AI generated a response letter, attached supporting documentation, cited IRS procedural guidance, and scheduled submission well before the deadline.

Marcus closed his laptop and went home.

Over the weekend, while friends complained about taxes and paperwork, Marcus barely thought about it. On Monday morning, he received confirmation that the response had been received. Weeks later, the notice was resolved with no adjustment.

But that wasn't the moment that stayed with him.

What stayed with him was what happened next.

Three months later, another letter arrived—this one regarding a penalty assessment tied to estimated taxes. Years ago, this would have sent Marcus into a spiral. This time, the AI already knew the issue before the letter arrived. It had tracked a midyear income surge and flagged that the IRS might assess a penalty even though Marcus qualified for safe harbor relief.

When Marcus uploaded the notice, the system was ready. It generated a penalty abatement request, referenced the correct safe harbor rule, and attached payment history as proof. The response went out the same day.

Penalty removed.

Over time, Marcus realized that the IRS had stopped feeling like an unpredictable authority and started feeling like a system—one that followed rules, responded to logic, and operated on data. And for the first time, he had a system that matched it.

Years passed. Marcus received fewer notices, not because the IRS had softened, but because his filings were cleaner, more consistent, and better documented. When notices did arrive, they were resolved quickly, often automatically.

One afternoon, Marcus noticed something remarkable. An IRS letter sat unopened on his desk—not because he was afraid, but because he knew it didn't matter when he opened it. The system would handle it either way.

He smiled, scanned it, and went back to work. For the first time in his life, an IRS letter didn't ruin his weekend.

And that quiet sense of control—that absence of fear—was worth more than any refund he had ever received.

Chapter 7

Future-Proof Compliance, Adaptive Tax Profiles & Staying Legal as Laws Change

Tax compliance has never failed because people wanted to break the law. It has failed because the law refuses to stay still. Rules evolve faster than habits, careers change faster than guidance, and financial lives shift faster than the IRS can explain how to stay compliant. What was legal yesterday may be restricted tomorrow. What was optional last year may be mandatory next year. Artificial intelligence introduces a new paradigm in tax compliance by making legality adaptive rather than reactive. Instead of asking whether you complied in the past, AI continuously ensures that you remain compliant as the law evolves.

At the center of this transformation is the adaptive tax profile. Traditional tax systems treat each year as a separate event. AI treats your tax life as a continuous timeline. Your income sources, filing status, investments, geography, family structure, and business activities are tracked as evolving variables rather than static entries. When a law changes, the AI does not wait for the next filing season to react. It recalculates how the new rule applies to your profile immediately. Compliance becomes a living state rather than a once-per-year checkbox.

This matters because most tax mistakes are caused by life changes colliding with rule changes. A new job, a side business, a move, an inheritance, a marriage, or an investment often triggers new reporting requirements that taxpayers do not realize exist. AI monitors these transitions automatically. When your profile crosses a legal threshold, the system responds instantly by updating forms, adding disclosures, adjusting withholding, or changing documentation requirements. You are not warned after the fact. You are guided before the mistake ever occurs.

Future-proof compliance also requires anticipating where enforcement is going, not just where it has been. AI systems learn from IRS behavior patterns, audit focus areas, and regulatory priorities. If enforcement begins shifting toward digital payments, gig income, crypto, or foreign accounts, AI adjusts risk scoring and compliance strictness accordingly. This allows taxpayers to align not only with the law as written, but with how it is likely to be enforced. Staying legal is no longer about blind adherence—it is about informed alignment.

AI also protects against compliance drift, a slow and dangerous phenomenon where taxpayers unknowingly move out of compliance over time. Small inconsistencies compound. Records degrade. Assumptions harden. AI detects this drift early by continuously validating current behavior against current law. If something begins to fall out of alignment, the system intervenes. Compliance becomes self-correcting rather than fragile.

Another critical element of future-proofing is jurisdictional complexity. As people earn income across states, countries, platforms, and asset classes, compliance becomes multidimensional. AI tracks which rules apply where, when, and to whom. It understands nexus, residency, sourcing rules, treaty implications, and reporting thresholds simultaneously. This eliminates blind spots that humans often overlook until penalties appear.

Perhaps most importantly, AI reframes compliance psychologically. When people feel permanently behind the law, fear dominates decision-making. When people feel synchronized with the law, confidence replaces fear. AI makes legality visible. It shows where you stand today, what will change tomorrow, and what actions keep you protected. The law stops feeling like a trap and starts feeling like a system you can navigate deliberately.

Future-proof compliance does not mean predicting every rule change. It means building a system that adapts automatically when change occurs. With AI, legality is no longer fragile. It evolves with you.

"The Year Nothing Went Wrong"

Noah used to believe that staying compliant was a matter of luck. Some years went smoothly. Others exploded without warning. A surprise bill. A penalty he didn't understand. A rule he didn't know existed until it was too late. He followed the news, trusted his accountant, and tried to do everything right, yet the system always seemed one step ahead of him.

The year he turned forty, everything changed—not because his finances got simpler, but because his compliance did.

Noah started the year with a single W-2 job and a modest investment account. By March, he had accepted a consulting role on the side. By June, he had moved across state lines for family reasons. By August, he had inherited a small portfolio of assets from an uncle he barely knew. In past years, this sequence of events would have guaranteed chaos. This time, the AI system noticed each change as it happened.

When the consulting income began, the AI updated his profile instantly. It adjusted withholding, generated estimated tax projections, and added the necessary schedules without Noah needing to ask. When he moved, the system recalculated residency rules, state filing obligations, and withholding requirements. Noah didn't fill out forms. He answered questions the system asked at exactly the right time.

The inheritance was the moment Noah expected everything to unravel. But instead of panic, he received a structured explanation. The AI showed him which assets triggered reporting, which ones didn't, how basis would be calculated, and what documentation would be required years from now—not just this year. His compliance profile expanded seamlessly, like a system designed to absorb complexity instead of break under it.

Midway through the year, tax law changed. Quietly. A reporting threshold was lowered. A disclosure requirement tightened. Most people wouldn't learn about it until tax season—if ever. Noah learned within hours. The AI flagged the change, explained its impact, and updated his compliance checklist automatically. No emergency. No scrambling. Just alignment.

What Noah didn't notice was just as important as what he did. There were no IRS letters. No notices. No penalties. No corrections. Not because he had fewer obligations, but because every obligation was met before it could become a problem.

At year's end, Noah sat down to review his taxes out of habit more than necessity. The return assembled itself. Every form was present. Every rule current. Every number validated. The system showed him not only that he was compliant, but why he would remain compliant even if the law changed again tomorrow.

Months passed. Then a full year.

Nothing went wrong.

No letters arrived. No corrections were required. No unexpected bills appeared. Noah realized something unsettling in its simplicity: this was what compliance was supposed to feel like. Quiet. Invisible. Predictable.

Years later, when friends complained about new tax laws and shifting rules, Noah listened politely. He understood their anxiety because he used to live inside it. But now, he lived inside something else—a system that moved with the law instead of lagging behind it.

The year nothing went wrong wasn't an accident.

It was the result of a system that adapted faster than fear ever could.

And once Noah experienced that level of control, he never looked at taxes—or the law—the same way again.

Chapter 8

The AI–IRS Interface: How Automated Systems Will Communicate, Decide & Enforce

The relationship between taxpayers and the IRS has always been shaped by asymmetry. The government has data, authority, and enforcement power, while individuals have limited information, delayed feedback, and little insight into how decisions are made. Artificial intelligence is fundamentally reshaping this relationship by creating a direct interface between taxpayer systems and IRS systems. Instead of humans communicating through forms, letters, and phone calls, algorithms increasingly speak to algorithms. Understanding this shift is essential because compliance is no longer just about following rules—it is about aligning with how automated enforcement systems interpret and act on those rules.

The modern IRS is rapidly becoming a data-first institution. Income, payments, asset transfers, and financial activity are reported automatically by employers, banks, brokerages, platforms, and payment processors. IRS AI systems ingest this data continuously, cross-check it, and flag discrepancies long before a human ever looks at a return. This means that by the time a taxpayer files, the IRS already has a probabilistic model of what that return should look like. AI-powered taxpayer systems are designed to mirror this process, ensuring that what you file aligns with what the IRS expects to see.

This alignment happens through structured data exchange. AI tax platforms format filings, disclosures, and documentation in ways that IRS systems can parse instantly. Numbers are not just reported; they are contextualized. Documentation is not just attached; it is indexed. Explanations are not narrative; they are procedural. This allows IRS algorithms to validate compliance faster, reducing delays, rejections, and unnecessary correspondence. In this environment, clarity beats persuasion. Precision beats explanation.

Another major shift is decision automation. Many IRS determinations—penalties, notices, corrections, and even some audit selections—are already being made without human intervention. AI taxpayer systems anticipate these decisions by running the same rule checks internally before filing. If an IRS system would flag a return, the taxpayer's AI sees it first. This creates a preemptive compliance loop where issues are resolved before enforcement is triggered.

AI also changes how disputes are handled. Traditional disputes rely on back-and-forth correspondence, long timelines, and subjective interpretation. AI-driven interactions rely on evidence, timestamps, and rule application. When both sides speak the same structured language, disputes narrow quickly. The question is no longer "What did you mean?" but "Which rule applies?" This dramatically reduces friction and uncertainty.

As IRS automation expands, compliance becomes less forgiving of ambiguity but more tolerant of precision. AI does not care about intent—it cares about alignment. This places a premium on systems that generate clean, consistent, well-documented data. Taxpayers who rely on memory, estimates, or informal explanations will increasingly struggle. Those who use AI systems designed to integrate seamlessly with IRS automation will experience faster resolutions and fewer disruptions.

The future of tax compliance is not adversarial. It is interoperable. AI does not eliminate enforcement; it makes it predictable. And predictability is the foundation of trust in any system. By understanding how AI interfaces with the IRS, taxpayers can move from defensive compliance to cooperative alignment—where filings are not just accepted, but expected.

"The Algorithm That Already Knew"

The notice arrived before Julian even realized there might be an issue. It wasn't threatening. It wasn't emotional. It was precise. A short message informing him that the IRS required clarification on a reported transaction involving digital assets. No accusations. No penalties. Just a request.

Years earlier, this would have sent Julian into a spiral. He remembered his first IRS letter vividly—the shaking hands, the rereading, the hours spent searching for answers online. This time, he felt something entirely different. Curiosity.

Julian uploaded the notice into his AI compliance system and watched as it unfolded the situation in real time. The system explained that the IRS algorithm had detected a mismatch between reported proceeds from a digital asset sale and basis information reported by an exchange. It wasn't an audit. It wasn't even suspicion. It was an automated request for alignment.

The AI already had the answer.

Months earlier, when Julian had transferred assets between platforms, the system had logged the transaction, preserved cost basis, and documented the movement. When he filed his return, the AI had flagged the transaction as compliant but noted that the IRS might request clarification due to delayed third-party reporting. The moment had arrived exactly as predicted. The system generated a response package automatically. Structured data. Supporting records. Timeline. Legal references. Julian reviewed it—not because he needed to fix anything, but because he wanted to understand how the system thought. It felt less like preparing a defense and more like completing a handshake between two machines.

When the response was submitted, Julian noticed something subtle but profound. There was no sense of pleading. No attempt to convince. The response simply aligned the IRS's data model with his own. Two systems synchronizing.

Weeks later, the case closed without comment.

What stayed with Julian wasn't relief. It was realization.

The IRS hadn't "found" something. It had detected a data variance. His AI system hadn't "argued" back. It had resolved the variance. No drama. No judgment. Just convergence.

As the year went on, Julian watched how often the system anticipated issues before they surfaced. A reporting threshold change triggered an updated disclosure. A platform reporting delay prompted early documentation. A regulatory update reshaped how future transactions would be logged. The system wasn't reacting to enforcement—it was coexisting with it.

One evening, Julian sat with his father, who was frustrated after receiving a confusing IRS notice. Julian listened patiently, then explained how his own system worked. His father shook his head slowly.

"So the IRS already knows," he said.

"Yes," Julian replied. "And now so do I."

That was the difference.

The fear his father felt wasn't about owing money. It was about being unseen, misunderstood, and powerless inside a system that spoke a language he didn't know. Julian didn't feel that fear anymore. He spoke the same language the system did—through AI.

Years later, as the IRS rolled out even more automation, Julian barely noticed. His system adapted silently. Filings went through faster. Notices became rarer. When communication did occur, it felt procedural, almost collaborative.

The algorithm already knew.

And because Julian's system knew too, nothing ever escalated.

In a world where enforcement became automated, clarity became protection.

And for the first time in the history of taxes, the power gap between the individual and the system had quietly begun to close—not through resistance, but through alignment.

Chapter 9

Human Judgment vs Algorithmic Precision: Where AI Draws the Line

No matter how advanced artificial intelligence becomes, tax compliance will never be entirely mechanical. The tax code is not purely mathematical; it is interpretive, contextual, and often subjective. Concepts like “ordinary and necessary,” “reasonable compensation,” “intent,” and “economic substance” are deliberately flexible, leaving room for judgment. This is where the boundary between human decision-making and algorithmic precision becomes critical. AI does not replace judgment—it structures it. Understanding where AI draws the line between automation and discretion is essential for using it responsibly and effectively in tax compliance.

AI excels at enforcing rules that are explicit. Thresholds, deadlines, phaseouts, caps, filing requirements, and documentation standards are applied flawlessly. Where the law is clear, AI is absolute. But where the law allows interpretation, AI shifts from enforcement to guidance. It identifies the range of legally defensible options, quantifies risk for each, and explains the implications. Instead of making a hidden judgment call, the system makes judgment visible.

This transparency is one of AI's most important contributions to tax law. Traditionally, taxpayers rely on professionals whose reasoning may never be fully explained. AI exposes the logic. It shows which IRS publications support a position, which court cases strengthen it, and how enforcement patterns affect risk. The taxpayer remains the decision-maker, but now operates with far more information than ever before.

AI also enforces consistency, which is often more important than aggressiveness. Many taxpayers run into trouble not because they push boundaries, but because they apply rules inconsistently over time. One year they claim an expense aggressively, the next year conservatively, without justification. AI tracks historical positions and flags deviations that could raise questions. This does not prevent change, but it requires explanation and documentation. Consistency becomes a strategic asset.

Another area where AI draws a clear line is intent. While AI cannot read minds, it can analyze behavior patterns. Repeated actions, timing, structuring, and documentation quality all signal intent to enforcement systems. AI evaluates these signals continuously. If a pattern begins to resemble avoidance rather than optimization, the system raises alerts. This protects taxpayers from drifting into risky territory without realizing it. AI also recognizes when automation should stop.

Complex scenarios involving novel transactions, ambiguous facts, or unresolved legal questions are flagged for human review. The system does not pretend certainty where none exists. Instead, it escalates decisions to the taxpayer or professional, supported by structured analysis. This hybrid model—automation with human oversight—is what makes AI sustainable and defensible in tax compliance.

As tax authorities increasingly rely on algorithms, understanding how those algorithms think becomes critical. AI-powered taxpayer systems act as interpreters, translating legal ambiguity into measurable risk and structured choice. The goal is not to eliminate judgment, but to prevent blind judgment.

In the end, AI draws the line where law meets interpretation. On one side lies precision, automation, and certainty. On the other lies discretion, strategy, and responsibility. When these two sides work together, compliance becomes not just accurate, but intelligent.

"The Choice the System Wouldn't Make"

When Evelyn sold her company, she expected complexity. She had spent years building it, reinvesting profits, structuring compensation carefully, and documenting everything. The exit was clean, legal, and well planned—but it wasn't simple. There were earnouts, deferred payments, equity conversions, and a gray area that made her uncomfortable the moment she saw it.

The AI system flagged the issue immediately.

It wasn't an error. It wasn't a violation. It was a choice.

The system explained that part of the transaction could be treated in two different ways under current tax law. One interpretation favored immediate taxation with lower long-term risk. The other deferred taxation but relied on a more aggressive reading of economic substance. Both were technically legal. Both had precedent. Neither was guaranteed.

What the system would not do was decide for her.

Instead, it laid everything out. Risk scores. Supporting cases. IRS enforcement trends. Probability ranges. Long-term projections. Evelyn sat at her desk late into the night, reading through explanations that were clearer than anything she had ever received from a human advisor. This wasn't advice disguised as certainty. It was clarity without pressure.

In the past, Evelyn would have deferred to someone else. Trusted their confidence. Followed their recommendation. This time, she realized the system was giving her something more valuable than certainty—it was giving her control.

She chose the conservative path. Months later, another founder she knew made the opposite choice in a similar deal. His tax bill was lower at first. Then the notice arrived. Then the audit. Then the years of correspondence. Evelyn watched from a distance as stress crept into his life, not because he had broken the law, but because he had crossed a line without realizing where it was.

Her system had known where the line was. It just hadn't forced her away from it.

Years passed. Evelyn's wealth grew steadily. Her filings remained clean. When new laws were introduced targeting transactions like hers, the system updated its analysis, confirming that her prior decision remained defensible. Nothing retroactive. Nothing threatening. Just quiet confirmation.

One evening, Evelyn revisited the original decision out of curiosity. She reread the analysis and realized something profound. The system had never tried to optimize for money alone. It optimized for sustainability.

She understood then why the system refused to decide. Judgment carried consequences beyond math. It carried emotional weight, long-term exposure, and personal tolerance for uncertainty. Those were human variables, not algorithmic ones. At a dinner party years later, someone asked Evelyn what the secret was to surviving a big exit without losing sleep. She smiled. “I didn’t let a system make my values for me,” she said. “I let it show me the truth, then I chose.”

In a world increasingly run by algorithms, Evelyn had discovered the quiet power of knowing exactly where automation ends—and where responsibility begins.

And that, she realized, was the safest place to stand.

Chapter 10

Permanent Compliance, Digital Identity & the End of Tax Anxiety

For generations, tax compliance has been episodic rather than permanent. People prepared returns once per year, reacted to notices after they arrived, and hoped that silence from the IRS meant everything was fine. This model was built for a paper-based world where information moved slowly and enforcement lagged behind activity. That world no longer exists. Artificial intelligence has ushered in an era of permanent compliance, where tax identity is continuously formed, evaluated, and validated in real time. Understanding this shift is critical because it marks the end of tax compliance as an annual event and the beginning of compliance as an ongoing digital state.

Permanent compliance means that your tax profile exists continuously, not just during filing season. Every income event, expense, asset movement, and financial decision contributes to a living record that evolves alongside the law. AI systems maintain this record automatically, updating rules, thresholds, and obligations the moment they change. Instead of retroactively explaining past behavior, taxpayers now operate inside a system that ensures legality as actions occur.

Compliance is no longer something you prove later—it is something you maintain by default.

At the center of this model is digital tax identity. This identity is not a username or account number. It is a structured representation of your financial life as understood by both taxpayer systems and government systems. It includes income patterns, documentation quality, reporting consistency, historical compliance behavior, and response reliability. Over time, this identity becomes predictive. IRS systems learn what compliant behavior looks like for you, and deviations become easier to detect—not because you are under suspicion, but because alignment has been established.

AI-powered taxpayer systems strengthen this digital identity by ensuring consistency across years, platforms, and jurisdictions. They prevent accidental contradictions, missing disclosures, and behavioral drift. They preserve documentation automatically and maintain legal continuity even as life changes. The result is a tax profile that becomes increasingly resilient over time. Each year of clean compliance reduces friction in future years. Notices decrease. Reviews resolve faster. Trust—algorithmic trust—accumulates.

This accumulation of trust has profound psychological consequences. Tax anxiety has never been about money alone.

It has been about uncertainty, invisibility, and lack of control. People fear taxes because they don't know where they stand until it's too late. Permanent compliance eliminates this fear by making status visible at all times. You know what you owe, why you owe it, and how it was calculated. You know what rules apply today and which ones will apply tomorrow. Anxiety fades not because taxes disappear, but because uncertainty does.

Another defining feature of permanent compliance is resilience to change. Laws will continue to evolve. Enforcement will continue to automate. New reporting regimes will emerge. AI-based compliance systems absorb these changes without disruption. They update logic, recalculate exposure, and adjust obligations silently. Taxpayers no longer scramble when rules change because compliance has already adapted.

Permanent compliance also reshapes accountability. In a digital environment, intent matters less than alignment. AI does not judge motives; it measures consistency. When behavior aligns with rules, compliance flows effortlessly. When misalignment occurs, correction happens early. This creates a system that is firm but fair, strict but predictable.

Ultimately, the end of tax anxiety does not come from lower taxes or simpler laws. It comes from visibility, continuity, and control. AI delivers all three. It transforms tax compliance from an annual source of stress into a stable background system that operates quietly and reliably. This is not the end of taxation. It is the end of fear-based taxation.

"The Quiet Year"

The first thing Thomas noticed was the silence.

No letters. No reminders. No late-night panic scrolling through forums. No sudden realization that a deadline had passed or a form had been missed. Just silence.

At first, it made him uneasy.

Thomas had lived his entire adult life in cycles of stress. Tax season loomed like a storm every year, no matter how organized he tried to be. Some years were better than others, but the pattern never changed. Anxiety built slowly, peaked violently, then faded—until the next cycle began. He had accepted this rhythm as normal.

Then he adopted a permanent AI compliance system.

At the beginning, nothing dramatic happened. His income flowed in. His expenses flowed out. The system asked occasional questions—brief, precise, timely. He answered them without urgency. The system updated quietly. Rules changed; he barely noticed. The year moved forward without friction.

By midyear, Thomas realized he hadn't thought about taxes in months.

This realization startled him more than any IRS notice ever had. He logged into the system expecting to find something wrong—some unresolved issue lurking beneath the surface. Instead, he saw clarity. His compliance status was green. His obligations were current. His documentation was complete. The system showed him exactly where he stood, not just now, but projected months into the future.

He remembered how different things used to feel. The guessing. The second-guessing. The dread that came from not knowing whether he was accidentally doing something wrong. That dread was gone.

Later that year, Thomas changed jobs. In the past, this would have triggered a cascade of errors—incorrect withholding, missed adjustments, surprise balances. This time, the system adjusted automatically. It recalculated everything in real time. There was no scramble. No correction. Just alignment.

When the law changed quietly in the fall—one of those changes most people wouldn't hear about until tax season—the system updated overnight. Thomas woke up to a notification explaining what had changed, how it affected him, and what, if anything, he needed to do. The answer was nothing. Nothing became a theme.

When filing season arrived, it felt anticlimactic. The return assembled itself effortlessly, drawing from a year of continuous compliance. There were no decisions to agonize over, no documents to hunt down, no numbers to reconcile. Filing felt like confirmation rather than creation.

After filing, the silence returned.

Weeks passed. Then months.

No letters came.

Thomas noticed something subtle but profound about this silence. It wasn't emptiness. It was stability. It was the absence of unresolved tension. The system hadn't made taxes disappear. It had made them predictable.

Years later, Thomas tried to explain this feeling to a friend who was still trapped in the old cycle of fear and reaction. He struggled to find the words. How do you explain the absence of anxiety to someone who has never known anything else?

"It's like living in a house where the foundation fixes itself," he finally said. "You stop checking for cracks."

That was the quiet miracle of permanent compliance. Not excitement. Not relief. Just a steady sense that nothing was about to go wrong.

And in that quiet year—free from fear, surprises, and second-guessing—Thomas realized something extraordinary.

For the first time in his life, taxes were no longer something he endured.

They were simply something that worked.

Final Thoughts

The End of Guesswork and the Beginning of Intelligent Compliance

Tax compliance has never failed because people were careless. It has failed because the system demanded perfection from humans in an environment built on complexity, constant change, and delayed feedback. For decades, taxpayers were expected to follow rules they could not see clearly, interpret laws they were never trained to understand, and respond to enforcement mechanisms they could not predict. Fear became normal. Confusion became expected. Overpayment became common. Artificial intelligence does not change the existence of tax law, but it permanently changes the relationship between individuals and the system that enforces it.

What this book has shown is that AI does not simplify taxes by removing rules. It simplifies taxes by mastering them. It reads every regulation, tracks every update, enforces every threshold, validates every number, preserves every document, and anticipates every enforcement trigger. In doing so, it transforms compliance from a reactive scramble into a stable, continuous state. This shift is not incremental. It is structural. Once compliance becomes permanent, visible, and automated, the psychological burden of taxation dissolves.

Throughout this book, you have seen how AI interprets tax law, updates compliance in real time, validates filings at IRS-grade standards, documents every decision, responds to notices with precision, adapts to legal change, interfaces directly with automated enforcement systems, respects the boundary between judgment and automation, and ultimately creates a permanent digital tax identity. Each chapter built toward a single conclusion: tax anxiety is not inevitable. It is a byproduct of outdated systems.

The future of taxation will not be defined by fewer laws or simpler codes. It will be defined by better systems. Enforcement will continue to automate. Reporting will continue to accelerate. The IRS will continue to rely on algorithms, data matching, and predictive models. In that world, compliance cannot rely on memory, habit, or annual effort. It must be continuous, structured, and intelligent. AI is not optional in this environment—it is foundational.

What makes this shift so powerful is that it restores balance. For the first time, individual taxpayers can operate at the same technological level as the institutions that govern them. Not through resistance or loopholes, but through alignment. When your system understands the law as well as the enforcement system does, compliance becomes cooperative rather than adversarial. Issues resolve faster. Audits become manageable. Notices lose their emotional charge. Silence becomes the norm, not the exception.

This book is not about avoiding taxes. It is about ending uncertainty. It is about knowing, at every moment, where you stand, what rules apply, and how your actions are interpreted. It is about replacing fear with visibility, stress with structure, and guesswork with precision. AI does not remove responsibility—it enhances it by making informed decision-making possible.

As you move forward, the question is no longer whether AI will shape tax compliance. That is already happening. The real question is whether you will continue to operate in a reactive, opaque system—or step into one that is adaptive, transparent, and resilient. The tools exist. The shift has begun. And once you experience permanent compliance, there is no going back to the old way.

Taxation will always be part of society. Anxiety does not have to be.

This is not the end of the series—it is the point where everything becomes sustainable.